Oven Honey
Typewriter Poems crafted at the Farm
by Dawn X. Spectre, 'The Amazing Alba"

Also by Dawn X. Spectre, "The Amazing Alba"

The Galloping Horse

Photography: Gloria Greene and Flora Farms

Back Cover Credits:
Gloria Greene, Owner of Flora Farms
Van Houten Maldonado, Devon (2015, March) Poetry for the
people. The News, thenews.mx/2015/03/poetry-for-the-people/.
 Reynolds, Christopher (2015, 22 February) Los Cabos, Mexico, is
largely back in business after hurricane. LA Times.latimes.com/travel/
mexico/la-tr-d-los-cabos-20150222-story.

Library and Archives Catalog Reference – typewriter poems, poetry,
organic farm, Los Cabos

For the late Enrique Monroy Pedroza, for leaving behind, not only my greatest gift, my son, but his immaculately cared-for 1955 Olympia Deluxe typewriter, and to all of you at the Farm, for allowing "The Amazing Alba" into your lives.

*Tanya Huntington and I met in Los Cabos and discovered some mutual interests including art and poetry. This introduction to Dawn X. Spectre, the typewriter poet, was written for my book presentation of **The Galloping Horse**, Abismos and Brown Bag Editorial, 2014 at Casa Refugio Citlaltépetl in Mexico City. It is my honour to include this esteemed author and artist's acute observations which provide a unique perspective on what it is I do.*
- "The Amazing Alba"- Dawn X. Spectre

Introduction: Dawn X. Spectre, Typewriter Poet
by Tanya Huntington

Ever since Plato tossed us out of the Republic, we poets have had to justify our existence and even more importantly, our income. Throughout the history of Western culture, our options have been limited to basically three: kissing the ring of some monarch, kissing the ass of some benefactor, or asking the government for a grant. Or have they?

Dawn X. Spectre – cloaked in the avatar "The Amazing Alba" seems to have found a, shall we say, more democratic way to avoid being a hunger artist: she hangs her shingle out in the open. Seated at a small table next to that ultra-technological device that allows one to draft texts and print them out instantaneously known as "a typewriter," she offers passersby custom-made verse much the same way that the scribes of Santo Domingo offer their assistance with legal paperwork –with the humble demeanor imposed by the streets, with the egalitarianism of chance.
To achieve this, "The Amazing Alba" must quickly don different masks while she is on the clock: that of Orpheus for elegies, that of Bashō for odes to Nature, that of Cyrano for matters of the heart –because her clients are well aware that poetry is, above all, good for one's love life. Unlike Robert Browning's duke, or the inhabitants of Spoon River channeled by Edgar Lee Masters, these *personae* are not formulated by the poet herself; they may arrive at any time and request any theme, thus adding a syncopated, improvised beat to her verse that echoes the keys striking the paper's surface.

The lyrical creations of Dawn X. Spectre are *sui generis*, made expressly to fulfill the poetic needs of every customer who happens by. Although she has never met the faithful Labrador back home, she calls him by name. Although she has no firsthand knowledge of that thirty-year marriage, she celebrates it. Although she does not believe in guardian angels, she invokes them wholeheartedly. And in exchange, her amorphous, variegated, unpredictable public provides "whatever they wish to contribute": a stamp of a patron saint, a bottle of wine, or on one memorable occasion, a one hundred-dollar bill.

Now it is up to us to lend her our eyes.

Tanya Huntington (U.S.A., 1969) is a writer and visual artist based in Mexico City. She holds a Ph.D. in Latin American Literature and teaches workshops in creative writing and literature at the Universidad del Claustro de Sor Juana. She has also produced and contributed to public radio and television programs on culture and art. Her current multidisciplinary art project, Mexican Nature, has been exhibited in the United States and Mexico and she is the author of the poetry book *Return/El regreso*, as well as the Managing Editor of *Literal: Latin American Voices* Magazine.

Dear Reader,

As Wordsworth once defined, "Poetry is the spontaneous overflow of powerful feelings: it takes its origin from emotion recollected in tranquility."

This collection of poems represents the written spontaneous overflow of feelings of the marvelous people that have passed through the portals of Flora Farms. Flora Farms is many things. It is a restaurant. It is a farm. It is cottages, desert and sea sounds, movie night and organic life. It is a seductive place to "recollect with tranquility."

I cannot begin to thank each and every one of you for your confidence in my art. One of you shared, "I just finished a workshop and we concluded that what people want is self-expression and connection with others." At the Farm I am known as "The Amazing Alba". I craft your random words or celebratory lauding and reflections on vintage paper, capturing a story. It is an interactive process and a public performance, where personal connections are made through the clacking of the keys, the texture of the paper, the ding at page end, and the facility of carbon paper.

My warm welcome at the Farm has enhanced my growth as a poet and a person. For being permitted to write amongst the splendour of the Farm, for the joy of the recipients, and so much more, I am grateful.

I feel all I have done up to this point in my life has been preparing me to write poetry in public.

To all of you who have encouraged me with your enthusiasm and belief in this thing that I do, I thank you.

Dawn X. Spectre
August 2015

Flora Farms, Los Cabos, Mexico.

TABLE OF CONTENTS

TABLE OF CONTENTS

Chapter One

Beginnings

Sunflower

Supported by long tall stalks
of friendship.

Leaves fluttering in breezes
of love.

Rooted
in kindness

we blossom,
as we follow the sun.

1

Spirits Flow

Around and around
our spirits flow.
I watch you with our offspring
you know.

The light in your eyes,
the water-sprite soul.
Your delight in the tiny hand
on the remote.

Chortling chuckles
among secret sheet-worlds of
free thought and infinite space,
limitless love and frontier-less fun.

Around and around
our spirits flow.
May it ever be so.

2

Buds Bloom

Inspired by passion's depth,
toiling in troubled times.
Driven by bright eyes,
excited expression, tamed aggression.

Tending fragile flowers,
stems burdened,
roots ripped out
or rotten.

They offer information,
kindness and soul,
helping one and other.

Buds bloom,
then flower.

3

Dawn X. Spectre

Warriors

It is an adventure every day,
warriors of the world of play.

Conquering first steps
and personal goals,

thriving in 'imaginatory' roles
developing skills,

defining good cheer
peace-makers leading without fear.

Jake and Mac

Jake and Mac
hit the waves.
The shore is far,
the current strong.
It pulls us along.
A little blown out,
still we laugh and shout,
build sandcastles when we get out.
You'll soon be able to view it on the big screen
'cuz Daddy filmed it scene by scene.

5

Dawn X. Spectre

In My Head

I like everything
that has a mechanical brain.

I like to see how things work
by putting them together first.

I like electronic toys
and robotic noise.

Diagrams, connections and plans,
I've got it all in my head.

And if I can't figure it out,
I look it up on the web.

6

Wonderful Like Me

I am a traveller.
I voyage to the sea.
I search and scan.
I dig in the sand.
And I discover…

the history of a land.
It appears
in broken fragments of bone,
in overturned stones.
I unearth the mystery
found by the sea.
And it's all wonderful,
wonderful, like me.

A Piece of Helado

I like to eat
what's sweet and cold.
I like to have it
in a cup to hold.
I like it in a cone too,
or just a little piece will do.

My Perfect Place

In my perfect place
I'd dine on candy every day.
Eat cupcakes with tea
then ice and whipped cream
topped with a cherry.
I'd snack on gum drops,
and shop with lollipops
and never, never would a cavity

get me.

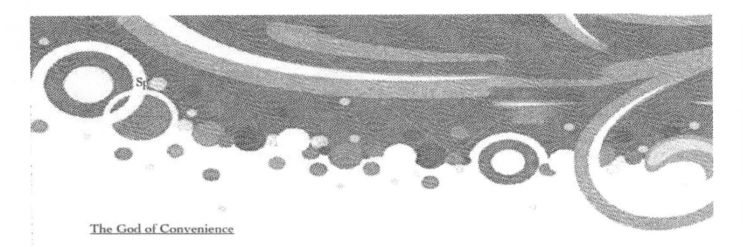

The God of Convenience

We are partial
to circular forms of food,
blended poultry parts
enshrined in crumbs.

We understand
it is not the most divine,
an offering to the god of convenience:
Lack Of Time.

Nevertheless
we smirk and smile in delight,
happily sated with each bite.

Cabo Vaca

It's Darcy on the beach
having fun with fantastic friends.

It's Riley on the move
top of the world, world of one.

It's Eva exploring
with snorkel and mask,

and McKenzie hanging around
trying to get a tan.

It's flip-flops and poses,
burnt body parts and noses.

Cabo vacation in the sun;
Fun, fun, fun, for everyone.

11

Dawn X. Spectre

A Winner Everyone

The ball bounces.
It gets slammed back
sometimes at your feet,
sometimes at the net.

It requires strength and speed,
a will to succeed.

On a court, school or home,
what you put in with persistence and fun,
makes a winner of everyone.

My Tia and Me

Brilliant butter-coloured
followers of the sun
dance gaily in the ocean breeze
nodding happily
under the coconut tree,

as my tia and me
discuss the complexity
of tranquility.

Dawn X. Spectre

Natural Born Leaders

In this day and age
we are the teachers,
independent and young
full of wisdom and fun.

We strive to combine
love divine with careers and
family time.

We are engineers,
and mystical seers.
Women - natural born leaders.

Along for the Ride

Much to my chagrin
I've watched you skin
a few elbows and knees
and other body parts in between.
    Your killer smile
    charming all;
    Daddy's blue eyes
    make the girls sigh,
    your creativity –
    so much a part of you
    just adds to
    your thoughtfulness
    and unique vision.
I can only guide,
go along for the ride,
try to help you make good decisions,
but in the end,
I'm counting on
your wisdom.

Dawn X. Spectre

Philadelphian Charm

We walk and discover
one and other, perusing pockets of
intrigue written on
historical plaques.

We move in concentric circles,
expanding outward,
each step taking us further apart,
while connecting our hearts.

Venturing into unknown territory,
learning as we go.
Step by step,
arm in arm,
mother – daughter,
intrepidly exploring
Philadelphian charm.

Leap High and Wide

Galloping through life
wind dreadlocking your hair.

Cantering through life,
well-seated, full of grace.

Trotting through life
smile on your face.

Walking through life
by my side, you are my pride.

May you meet every obstacle in stride -
leap high and wide.

Chapter Two

Passion

It's Early

It's early in the game,
and I just wanted to say,
though it may be old school,
 - I think you're cool.

You are creative and sweet,
with you, new things are neat.

Is it written in the stars?
It's still early in the game.
I was just wondering,
do you feel the same?

Dawn X. Spectre

Tick Tock

Tick tock goes the clock.
Time is passing,
our friendship is lasting.

It might be too soon
but I think it's opportune.

I wonder if you would
like to accompany me
to the upcoming
Sadie?

That Guy

I am not a wordsmith
nor a crafter of fine verse,
but I can touch your arm and
be smitten by your charm.

I am not a poet.
I would never claim to be,
but I can whisper sweet nothings,
meaningfully.

I can make you smile,
or at least I can try,
can chat and hear you laugh,
and listen to your - ideas.

I can practice kindness.
I can try to be
that guy –
count on me.

21

Dawn X. Spectre

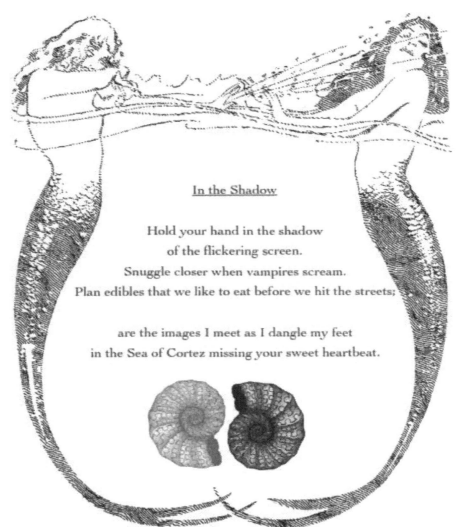

In the Shadow

Hold your hand in the shadow
of the flickering screen.
Snuggle closer when vampires scream.
Plan edibles that we like to eat before we hit the streets;

are the images I meet as I dangle my feet
in the Sea of Cortez missing your sweet heartbeat.

The Sweetness They Make

It's a good thing
I'm sweet on you,
'cuz I've been cut off
from sugar and pies,
and all that's fine.

It's a good thing,
for Meilani and Ben,
that all the syrup, candy and cake
cannot equate
with the sweetness that they make.

Dawn X. Spectre

Passion True

Whether it is bitter or semi-sweet,
its power is complete.

It can jumpstart your engine.
It can sweep you off your feet.
It's a Mexican tradition,
rooted in Mayan lore.
The magic core
of complicit charms.

Its delicacy reminds me of you,
passionate and true.

24

<u>Bam!</u>

Love takes you full force.

A five course meal;
appetizers
      of adoration,
salads
      of kindness,
main course
      of love and respect,
topped off
      with the pièce de résistance –
      trust.

Buen Provecho!

Dawn X. Spectre

Happy

Happy is what you make me,
every single day.

The sun on cloudy mornings
reflected in your eyes.

Your wise interpretation
of other people's lives.

The care that you take -
you keep me awake!

You are the vowels in my alphabet,
without them I make no sense.

And I cannot fail to mention,
that fatal attraction,

the cherry on the cake
that makes me ache,

that highlights all the rest,
are your amazingly, lovely, large,

breasts.

Karmic Beginnings

We are butterflies
flitting from each sturdy stem
observing all
from the heart.

Captured in a spectral symphony,
kaleidoscope colours
surround our serenity.

Baja bounty blesses
karmic beginnings.

27

Dawn X. Spectre

By You

I drown in your
sweet as sarsaparilla eyes.

I tremble in the reverberations
of your sultry voice and sighs.

Am cuddled by
your cozy chuckles,

senses heightened,
burdens lightened,

by you.

Etched in Love

Shape-shifted walls
mark longer absences.
Toothpaste capped, welcome mat,
subtle surprises tease;
aimed to please.

His magic touch,
evident and plain,
etched on my heart,
even when apart.

Etched in love,
here, there and anywhere.

Dawn X. Spectre

Caress Each Chord

Busy laughing with you
might make you think that I don't see
how much you mean to me.
Your easy-going sanctity
makes the world so much friendlier.
Your cheesy jokes suit most folks,
inspire a positivity,
create harmony.
Like your loving hands full of talent
as they caress each chord,
engage my core and
lightly strum
my inner soul.

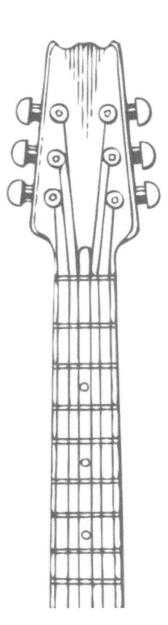

30

World on Fire

Run-ragged rages
ripping through stages.
World on fire.

Lust burning up space,
searing skin.
World on fire.

No time to rest,
no time to tire.

Gotta stay up.
Gotta stay wired.
World on fire.

Dawn X. Spectre

<u>Love on the Run</u>

Ever been to The Office?
It's where anything can happen.

The confluence of improbability
is stimulated
by the proximity
of topless chicas
and promiscuity.

It's not an ideal place
to open your heart.
It's just a start
to fun, love on the run,
and doing whatever
turns you on.

The Funky Pheasant

Watching the fabulous funky pheasant
in his polymer shirt,
at Flora Farms was a hoot.

Boogying with a gaggle of giggling gals,
he created quite a kerfuffle
when he waddled up to Bruce
in his birthday suit.

33

Dawn X. Spectre

<u>Weekend Getaway</u>

It's a weekend getaway.
A chance to say
that life's too short.
A chance to play
in love's resort;
to explore lushness
amid arid accolades.
To smile and float in
cheeriness.
Take a chance
on romance.

Gentle Climes

I would love to accept
your kindly attentions.
I won't promise
to be your keeper,
your problem solver,
your rock.

I just want to share
some ephemeral care.
Explore libido laden lust
and satisfying strolls
in gentle climes.

Dawn X. Spectre

Tequila Neat

Discovering new frontiers
with you
there's no fear.

It's all fission and heat
on beaches; tequila neat.

First time enhanced
south of the border romance.

<u>What if…</u>

What if
I lay down in a bed of rose petals
when all you want is one.

What if
I ply you with kisses,
when one will do.

What if
I asked you to be my wife.
Would I be the one,
the one for you?

Dawn X. Spectre

I'll Meet You There

Time after time,
I've watched you present and attentive.
He brings out a new you.

Fission with decision,
it looks like love.
You know:
 a connection, everlasting,
an understanding that's not demanding.

Is it possible after all these years,
you'll be striding tall and proud,
down the aisle?

Time will tell.
Pick a spot,
I'll meet you there.

Three Little Words

Our love is new.
Could it be true?
We need to give
it a chance.
Let go of fears.
We know it's here.
I'm stuck on you.
Mario approves too.

Can we do it?
Can we say IT?

Those three little words,
that lead to two –
"I do."

Dawn X. Spectre

Fruta Fresca

Fruta fresca
in the groove.
Hands held solidly,
me and you.

Born on the same date,
ruby agate.
Twelve great years,
life-perfect pieces,
we fit.

There is no puzzle.
There is no mystery.
Our love has a
fabulous history.

Nothing will change.
It's fate. It's love true,
even if we say,
"I do."

The First Dance

If Libby and Ziggy could talk
(and they do)
they would say they have found
of all people, the best two.

 A pair of sweethearts
since high school days
wielding happiness
in so many ways.

This love of a lifetime -
a true one and only
that few ever encounter
are ready to take the next step
in a textbook romance.

The white dress,
the first dance,
forever (Boog to the max)
yours and mine.

Dawn X. Spectre

Gorgeous and H.O.T.T.

Gorgeous and H.O.T.T. hot,
are going to tie the knot.

They have not hurried.
They are not worried.
They're on the right track.
Stanford studies secured;
Theta fun and 'The One'.

In wedded bliss,
they surely cannot miss.
In San Francisco,
in Lake Tahoe
in love.

Alley to Aisle

It has to make you smile
to know that someone you meet,
discreetly on the street,
could take you so far -
could take you to the stars.

In the great plan,
a couple found
each other,
combined strength and sensitivity
balance out for David and Stephanie.

Big-mouthed,
adventurous and full of fun,
in November you will smile,
when they walk down the aisle,
full of charm on the farm,
in paradise.

Dawn X. Spectre

Wedding Time

If you could choose a wife
to spend with your entire life,
you'd elect a lady
who is known for her geniality.

You'd look for someone
genuine and smart,
creative and kind,
the best friend that you can find.

Edgar, though always on the run,
has found that certain someone.
Not only is she all of the above,
she's a beauty and as well, a great mom.

Loving, giving parents, they've really got it all.
And soon they will marry,
consolidating their fortune fine,
in August, it's wedding time.

Boss Lady

It's all about the fireworks
the sauce and spice
to excite
in a new life, settlers in spite
of what some say is right.

Boss lady,
I'll follow your lead.
Don't even have to plead.
It's all about the need
to live our lives
as they're meant to be.

Dawn X. Spectre

Date Night

In this place
that we are in life,
it seems we share
more with others
than we ought.

That makes this date night,
more than nice - it makes it great.

A chance to look into your eyes
with heartfelt sighs
and remember,
we too have lives.

Down to Earth

Down to earth
sedate yet awake,
they like the finer things in life
to alleviate the strife.

Maintaining a certain sense
of what is best,
they settle in, glass in hand,
an Irish whiskey and
a fine Bourbon blend.

Dawn X. Spectre

The Quieter Moments

Skipping about the planet,
defining the what's and where's,
it is easy to forget
that it means little,
without someone to share,
the quieter moments.
Just us two,
where love is true.

Je T'Adore

Sympathetic eyes that adore.
Gentle sighs that explore.
Travel and adventure that soar
on wings of amor.

Je t'adore.

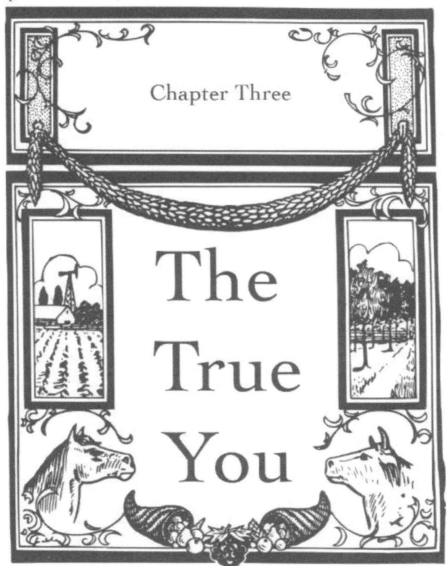

Chapter Three

The
True
You

Master of Your Destiny

Strength and rectitude
radiate
from your perch
in the sky
as you survey
the dawning of a new day,
tranquil as the winter sea,
master of your destiny.

Dawn X. Spectre

Sailor's Creed

Sail luffing
in the light breeze.
Timelessness
in a constant sea.

Sail full
moving fast.
Adrenalin rushes.
Time passes.

Focus on the horizon.

Ocean Vagabond

Your snub-nosed confidence
wields you through
the open sea.
Travelling where you please,
Independence a need,
taking care of family.

Charming, strong,
ocean vagabond.

Dawn X. Spectre

Journey

It's all about the journey,
knowing what to do.

Just as important as being true,
to who you are.

It is time for a break,
a 'get serious' take.

Meet the you
you know you can be.

Pack it all in a box,
take a chance, it might rock.

And if not
at least you gave it a shot.

Transition

Resistance to change
is contrary
to nature.

Untended
vitality
stuck in
static time
invites
transition.

Dawn X. Spectre

Rainbows and Glitter

It is rainbows and glitter.
Eyes wide open,
time to reconsider
the definition
of personal gain.

Go against the grain
of what one is used to.

As with all change,
it comes with pain,
and leaves one refreshed
with the bequest
of a life lived,
not driven.
Rainbows and glitter.

<u>I Like to Dream</u>

I like to sit in my

comfy chair,

and lose myself in foreign air -

found between the pages

of a book.

I don't like to think about

the why's and what's.

I like to dream and write

invitations on my

Royale typewriting

machine.

Dawn X. Spectre

On the Cusp

There is always one,
one good –
to take you to
heights unknown
to complement
the face all know.

But it is true
there is always one,
one bad –
to take you
where you would never go,
to help you see
what never shows.

No Longer Blind

I wake up
in wonderland
transplanted.

 Let air in,
lungs expanded,
oxygen high.

Open my eyes,
no longer blind.

Adaptability

Incorporate the unexplained.
Create a space for the unplanned.

Open hidden doors
to the unknown.

Go with the flow,
let negativity go.

Instant integrity.

Scorching Truths

Touch a fire,
get burned.

Simple theory
complicated task
amid,
tramped on souls,
mangled messages,
myriad signs,
and scorching truths.

Quiet enlightenment heightens
alert acceptance.

VESTA.

61

Dawn X. Spectre

Flower Power

Under the setting sun,
the crash of waves and slipping sand
drowns out the sound
and surrounds the land.

It sends a breeze
to brighten our vista and
ignites our lives
with spots of colour –

flower power.

62

For All You Do

A life of service
is no easy job.
It's an ability
to defeat
negativity and tired feet.

It requires an inner sense of strength
that honours,
even people you might
not like.

Its rewards are plentiful
and often invisible,
but its karmic worth
is infinitely immeasurable.

Dawn X. Spectre

Soul Catharsis

String words together
in trendy patterns.
Sound out designs;
imagery of the mind.

Expressed on a page,
in love or rage.
The universe in evolution,
lends a voice to illusion.

Budding Flower

I am a budding flower.
There is much of me left to unfold.

Respond to light,
seek the shade.
Afraid
to reveal the bounty I hold.

Not so hard to express for others,
yet quite a feat,
to let you meet,
to really see,
the person
I call me.

Dawn X. Spectre

<u>House in Order</u>

Once convinced,
it takes a plan,
perhaps a friend, or two
with whom to stand.

Eliminate the temptations
that pollute.
Healthy juice, exotic fruit
chase the toxic stain.
Clean the brain.

House in order.

Seize the Day

It is a question of
you are what you eat.
Organic vegetables are
not a treat.

They are chock full of taste.
Eliminate the toxic waste.

Help you to see
the beauty of life today.

Seize the day.

Dawn X. Spectre

The Love Inside

I am not a quitter.
So do not worry
if we do not see
eye to eye.
It is not good-bye.

I just have to find
common ground and rely
on the love
we hold inside.

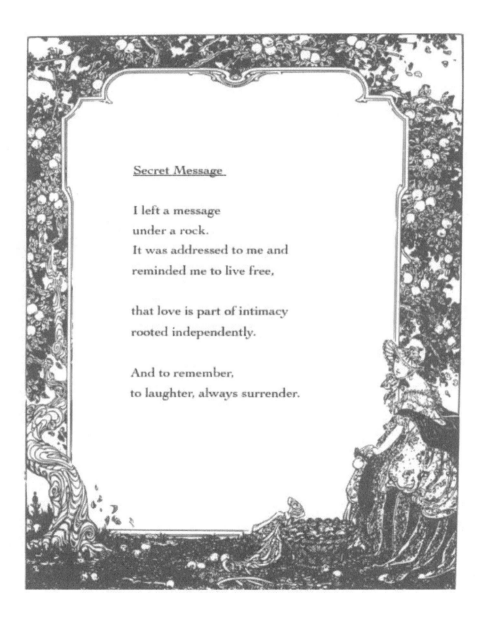

Secret Message

I left a message
under a rock.
It was addressed to me and
reminded me to live free,

that love is part of intimacy
rooted independently.

And to remember,
to laughter, always surrender.

Dawn X. Spectre

Piano and Me

I carry on my fingers
a whole symphony defined.
A collection of interpretations,
rhythmic expressions of my mind.

The chordal combinations
like vertebrate of the spine,
caress and flow
in tiempos; four, six, eight and nine.

My baby grand and
portable with stand;
appendages infused,
sound-defined
lifeline.

Good Enough

I've a gift
that happens to be
an ability to play
just three chords;
a musical entity.

I've a gift
that happens to include
broken phrases and
quirky interludes
that neither flow nor dance.

I've a gift
that sets the barrier
at a level that is free.
It grabs the imagination,
not Bono, Prince or John-ny,
but hey, it's good enough for me.

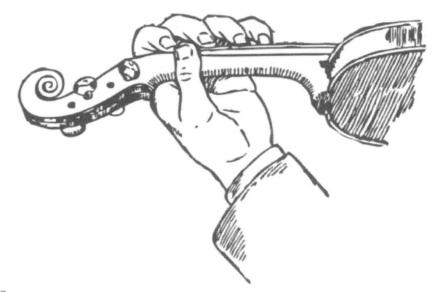

Dawn X. Spectre

In Your Presence

It is an honour
to know you.
The Club comes alive
in your presence.
Brothers Ronnie and Donnie
and the other brother, Daryl;
Handsome and kind,
not hard on the eyes.

May your beer always be cold.
May you never think 'old',
and if I may be so bold,
May I just say,
It's been great, it's been gold.

72

Solid

You are the master of disaster.
You're the twisted sister
of the dudes – mister.

You're so solid bro' you bounce.
Shitstorm trance - not a man romance.

Just for laughs, friends and fun,
tequila in the sun.

73

Dawn X. Spectre

A Hundred Miles

Parched throat virtuoso
stranded at the hundred mile mark
mutters the only Spanish
he ever knew.

Frozen in frosted bottles
appears the formula,
alongside the tacos de cabeza,
illusive interims of intimacy,
a hundred miles from
every place.

Scents of Grace

Struggling with his heroin-stoked
vision, his arrogance provoked
long films of sounds
heard through Herbie's ears.
Frantically signing his distaste,
he utters blasphemies,
heckling scents of grace.

Master manipulator,
mute by election,
ignorant by choice,
his street performance,
paid his mansion residence
where he stews
in his own misuse
supporting eco-projects
and medicinal investigations.

75

Dawn X. Spectre

<u>Track of Life</u>

Train runs down the track.

clickity clack

Flip on the internal screen.
Watch the scenes
of happiness.

clickity clack

Forged from family ties
and friends that stand by.

clickity clack

Interventions of connections

clickity clack

down the track

clickity clack

of life.

Chapter Four

Wisdom

The Bounty of Years

I n wonder we watch and learn.

N ot without wily wishes

S urprised, we are daily witnesses to the

P reciousness, the bounty of years brings.

I ndividual souls who

R emind us and inspire us to

E xcellence.

Dawn X. Spectre

Sweet as Canadian Corn

Wild woman
taming the skies,
taming the land
where family descend.

Good soul,
sweet as buttermilk pancakes
on a Sunday morn,
sweet as Canadian-grown corn.

A lifetime ventured,
a family gained.
Queen of the sky,
lets you soar
now, before and forever more,
immensely adored.

It's Hereditary

Shrouded in mystery
even after all our history.
I couldn't believe
you kept a secret.

And no little 'cosa',
but a 'grandiosa'.
The grandest honour:
when Ashley named her daughter,
after me.

Of course
this safely secures
that she'll be charming and strong.
That she'll get along
with just about everybody.
Just like her role model -
It's hereditary.

Dawn X. Spectre

Soon?

Formed in a foundation,
based on fun, service and wine.
The greatest couple around
have withstood time.

Raised two prize sons,
and settled down to a rhythm of one.
Fun-loving Beagle caregivers for now
waiting in expectation of
future generations,
new trials and tribulations
...soon to follow?

Don't Tempt Fate

I don't mean to be unkind.
I am just worried about your
fast-tracking, high-clicking mind.

Though the pleasure of flesh
can often tempt us,
it is prudent
to uncover common ground,
where ideas can be sounded
about stuff that really matters.

Regardless of who flatters,
I just want to say,
a playmate is okay,
but if it's for all days,
look for someone who can relate.

Don't tempt fate.

83

Dawn X. Spectre

<u>Hard to Know</u>

Sorrow seeps into every
silver-lined cloud.

It permeates a crowd;
closes doors, enshrouds.

To move on is to let go.
Easy to say, hard to know.

Oven Honey

Empty Nester

Put everything in its place.
Wrap the elastics into a ball.
Re-paint the hall.

The list of things grows tall
as we settle in
to tranquility
and worrisome waits.
(Will they ever call?)

Solace in the sound
of TV's and doorbells,
and neatly stacked magazines of
travel plans.

85

Dawn X. Spectre

<u>Lost</u>

I am lost
in this world
without you.
Ripped from my soul
each day takes its toll.

I try and move on.
In time it may ease,
but now, it is all I can do;
to smile and please those who mean well.

Maybe tomorrow, maybe not at all
but until then I'll just say,
it's a never-ending living hell.

Companions

Murphy and Cassidy
travelled with me far.

Guiding with their compassion,
they captured my heart;
enlarged its capacity,
made it start.

Companions to the end,
we continue together,

wandering the rainbow bridge,
here and hereafter.

Dawn X. Spectre

Stronger not Stranger

It is all too soon to stop the flow.
the give and take, the get up and go.

Partners inclined to living life,
grateful in receipt of each kindness.
Scared, scarred, stronger not stranger.

Partners inclined to living life,
grateful for a healthy wife.

In Gratitude I Gaze

I don't think about it a lot,
the struggle to do with naught.
The struggle to get it right
to protect the planet
and practice random acts of nice.

I don't think about it a lot
because of what we've got.
A family that makes a difference,
a balance few can equate.

As hardship fades, I value its base.
In gratitude, I gaze into your eyes
thankful for this well-earned grace.

Dawn X. Spectre

Recovery

Splat.
Interact.
Wind and storm
ripped out and torn.

Majesty toppled.

And righted.
Patrick ought to be knighted.

Reintegrated;
out with the old,
in with the new.

Recovery
re-discovery of
family, faith, and friends.

Master Plan

Bound by the forces of nature,
struck by her fury
she sounds out the alarm.

Failed to charm
the shoddy constructs;
man's follies
pushed to the side.

All that's left
is what began.

Recovering,
discovering,
Mother Earth's
master plan.

91

Dawn X. Spectre

Afterword by Dawn X. Spectre

The title of this collection of poems, *Oven Honey*, was inspired by Gloria and Patrick Greene, owners of Flora Farms. Oven honey is defined by *The Glossary of Words in Use in Cornwall: West Cornwall by Miss Courtney 1880 as* "*dregs* of the honeycomb which are drawn out of the honeycomb when placed in a warm oven."

Oven Honey is a collection of moments which extend over the course of a year starting in June 2014 through to the end of May 2015. These "spontaneous overflows of emotions" are all moments I have shared with guests and staff at the Farm. They are 'drawn out' and transformed into the poems which make up this book. Just as a painting does not require a title to be understood, it is my hope that these poems can stand alone leaving the reader to create one's own images from these free-verse word snapshots.

Having said that, I have been encouraged to share some of the details of the poem's inspirational beginnings and you will find some notes below. This collection of "poetry for the people", as the journalist Devon Van Houten Maldonado described my work in *The News - Mexico City*, is divided into four chapters revolving around the four seasons, the four elements, the four directions, and the four stages of life.

Beginnings

The poems in this first chapter are about children and children at heart, the springtime of life, starting out and plants sprouting. *Beginnings* is represented by the Eastern compass, life's season of spring and the element of air.

"Spirits Flow" is a poem written at the request of the mother for the father of their child while the couple was experiencing adjustment to this new life in their lives.

"Buds Bloom" was written for a private school principal with all my admiration for the hard work that educators do in providing what a child needs in order to bloom.

"Warriors" through "The God of Convenience" are poems written at the request of children. In my process I ask people what they would like a poem about. That is a scary question to most, so I make it easier by suggesting they tell me a story or just throw out random words. I love random word poems. Children offer some of the most creative inspiration as they are excited to direct me to make them something that is uniquely theirs and are less inhibited about what is 'suitable' poem subject material. "The God of Convenience" was a random word poem for a young man who was stymied and thought he had nothing to say. Finally I asked him what his favourite food is and with mischievous eyes in this delectable organic fine-dining establishment, he said chicken nuggets.

Passion

Passion is the summer season of life, young adulthood. Passion is hot. Its element is fire and its compass point is represented by the South. These are the poems of passion which are nurtured and abound daily at the Farm. There are many testimonies to love and the longing for marriage and love in all shapes and forms. I am so impressed by the amount of love that enters the Farm.

93

Dawn X. Spectre

Husbands, boyfriends, girlfriends, wives, mothers, daughters, sons, family and lots of friends - come in gangs from LA and NY and beyond, delighting in each other and the passion that also goes into every inch of the Farm.

"Tick Tock" was inspired by a young girl's quest for a date at the upcoming Sadie Hawkins dance. For those of you unaware, this is a youth's tradition where the girl asks a boy to a school dance that originated in a comic strip.

"That Guy" was written by a waiter in pursuit of a new love.

"What If" made me nervous as the gentleman was considering marriage and it is a tentative proposal.

"The Sweetness They Make" is a about a couple in love who had both decided to diet.

"Happy" is the only poem in which I have been asked to use that final word. The man who asked for the poem was, at first, disappointed in the pictures I painted with words, probably expecting a saucy limerick. He had asked for a poem about his love using those last two words. I explained that the other words were metaphors of his love and in the end, both members of the couple were very happy.

"Gentle Climes" was written for a mature lady who explained to me she was interested in a man but only for a little fun and did not know how best to tell him.

"Three Little Words" and "Fruta Fresca" were two Valentine's Day poems written for two marriage-hopeful women who are best friends. The two women had very different stories but each with the same marriage goal. One had just recently met her beau and was anxious to tie the knot while the other had been in a long-term relationship with hers and was also ready to take the next step.

"Alley to Aisle" is a true story of a lovely couple with a great sense of humour that really met in an

94

alley and is booked to get married at the Farm.

"Date Night" is a poem that I am sure reflects the life of many couples whose lives revolve around tourism and the service industry. This particular couple worked as a captain and mate team on a boat.

"The Quieter Moments" is similar in theme and perhaps a common one for many of the famous people who pass through the gates of the Farm. I never met the couple for whom this poem was written. I was merely told to write a love poem for a busy couple who had recently married. It wasn't until after I finished the poem that I put two and two together about which couple the poem was for. The names will remain anonymous in keeping with the poem's message.

Psyche – The True You

In this chapter, the westerly point in the autumn of life represents the unsettling and settling of discovering and growing into the 'you' who you truly are. These poems are about life's lessons, learned. It is a powerful time where one finally feels at one with one's self; the master of one's own destiny. The poems are stories or random words that explore the soul-searching explorations.

"Master of Your Destiny" was a poem I created after being handed a piece of paper with the words destiny, tranquil, sea, eagle. This poem just flew out of my pen.

Flower power, sun, sand, and sea were the words given by a family for the poem "Flower Power". The mother of the family did not like the flower power phrase, but in fact it offered me a new version, of the oft mentioned theme of sun, sand and sea celebrated in this paradise we call Los Cabos.

The origin of "Budding Flower" surprised me as the person who asked for it uncovered timidity that, as a professional performer, she never exudes. It came from a glimpse into the musician's artistic angst.

The Farm attracts the healthy, as reflected in "House in Order", written for a woman who was dining out for the first time since abstaining from alcohol.

Acceptance comes in the form of music such as in "Piano and Me" which reflects the oneness of this professional pianist with his instrument. He asked me for a poem about his piano, which if you have seen him perform, you would know is a part of him.

In "Good Enough for Me", a different musical theme came from the poem request from this good-natured amateur musician. His jocular attitude did not hide the rocking rebel inside completely, but his sensitive side was pleasantly surprised after our conversation about music and musicians, with what I came up with.

"In Your Presence" was petitioned for by an employee who had left her job at 'The Club' and wanted to express how much she would miss the members. She was much loved and this poem was enthusiastically received.

The theme "What doesn't kill you makes you stronger," can be found in "A Hundred Miles" and "Scents of Grace" which were Beat poet type requests; the petitioners being just as excited with word pictures as I am. These poems were easily written with the iconic melodies of The Shaman's, the Farm house band, playing in the background.

The closing poem in this chapter, "The Track of Life" is both a conclusion to life's autumn season and a precursor to its winter. The reason I chose trains as a subject is that the petitioner of this family-gratitude poem told me they were from an American 'railroad family'.

Wisdom

The winter season is represented by the north. The poems in *Wisdom* represent culmination, the element of Earth, and the 'ashes to ashes' contemplation of the wisdom that Earth's bounty offers.

The "Bounty of Years" was written for a wonderfully warm Retirement Center coordinator and her staff who were on vacation together in Los Cabos.

"Sweet as Canadian Corn" is homage to a petitioner's grandmother, a pilot, from what I believe was the 1940s, and surely a very special woman with many more stories.

I loved my conversation with the candid grandmother who asked for the poem, "Don't Tempt Fate". She was truly concerned that this "nobody" that her granddaughter was involved with was a big mistake. She said she understood that fooling around for the short term was okay, but not for the long term, and thought the poem was a good way to get that idea across.

In this wise chapter we meet loss, the Odile hurricane and healing. For healing is what one does surrounded by the magic of Flora Farms; a modern day version of *The Secret Garden*, the 1911 children's classic by Francis Hodgson Burnett. "Lost" is an elegy from a mother whose two young adult children met incomprehensible deaths. The concluding poem, "Master Plan", was requested from the reporter Christopher Reynolds, a poem about Hurricane Odile. One of the first I wrote on the subject, having just recently dug out of its trail of wrath. The poem got me a mention in the *LA Times* article about post-Odile Los Cabos and was published in newspapers throughout North America. (Thank you, Christopher.)

I am sincerely grateful to all of you for sharing your words and stories with me during these special moments and to the Greene's and their fabulous staff for their continued support.

Dawn X. Spectre,
San Jose del Cabo, August 2015
dawnsxpectre@gmail.com

Made in the USA
Columbia, SC
10 December 2022

72326129R00067